W9-AHF-503

The Beginner's Guide to Dwarf Hamster Care

A Simple, Practical Guide To Raising A Happy Dwarf Hamster

By
DEXTER WARREN

TABLE OF CONTENTS

5

THE DWARF HAMSTERS

S o, Snow White may have had her seven dwarfs. But they don't compare at all to the four dwarfs we're about to discuss in this book. And no their names aren't even near Dopey, Doc, Happy, Sleepy, Sneezy . . . well you get the idea.

What we're talking about here is a delightful "pocket pet." A small little furry creature that'll win your heart the moment you take a look at him: The dwarf hamster.

For those of you who aren't familiar with the dwarf hamster, you may be a little surprised that there are a variety of hamster out there that's even smaller than the Syrian or Golden Hamster.

A Syrian hamster is about eight inches in length – a little guy in his own right by any definition. So just how small does a hamster have to be to be thought of as a dwarf.

These guys get no bigger than four inches in length. They're actually so small that they can climb right through the spaces between a regular wire hamster cage!

Now that's tiny! But the love and delight they'll provide your family is huge. If you've been considering adding a pet to your family, but just don't have the room for a dog or even the space for a cat and accompanying litter box, consider the addition of a dwarf hamster to your family.

But we'll warn you right now: While they're small, they are not without their needs, just like any living pet. You'll find though that spending time caring for these guys, playing and interacting with them will provide you with some of the best moments of your day!

A Member (Albeit Cute)
Of The Rodent Family

Don't let this negatively influence you, but hamsters are members of the rodent family.

Yes, the same family that brings you rats –
and those cute cuddly mice.

On the plus side, it's the same family of
which the adorable guinea pig is a member
as well.

Seems like that's a contradiction in terms.
How could something so small be
considered wild?

The truth is there are no dwarf hamsters
left in the wild. These little guys have been
strictly bred to be pets – and they serve
their purpose well. But they do have a
cousin who – much the chagrin of some
Asian farmers – are still roaming free today.

Common hamster is mostly how these wild
rodents are called. While he's not on the
verge of extinction, his numbers are
definitely dwindling. But if you expect him
to look anything like the dwarf hamster
you're considering adopting, you'll be
surprised to learn he's not anything like
that.

The common or wild hamster has an almost
raccoon-like coat of black and brown. At
one time he was easily found throughcut

Russia and Central Europe. But his penchant for vegetables like Peter Rabbit and his love of Farmer Macgregor's garden patch has made him increasingly scarce in those parts of the world.

But you can find wild hamsters in other parts of the world as well, including Africa, Asia and even parts of Western Europe. And some of these varieties – unlike most dwarf hamsters – even have tails. For example, the wild Chinese hamster – like his domesticated namesake – has a tail, as what people call the mouse like hamster, found in the Middle East.

Another specie of wild hamster, at home in South Africa, have white tails and hence are referred to most often as "white-tailed hamsters."

Tracing Hamster History

So how did a desert rodent – detested and despised by farmers – transform its reputation into a cute, cuddly and simply loveable pocket pet (so named because these guys can literally fit in your pocket!)

I'm glad you asked.

Let's go back in time to the 19th century –
specifically 1829. That's the year George
Waterhouse, a British zoologist, stumbled
across one of these small creatures in the
Syrian city of Aleppo.

For reasons unknown, he called the rodent
Cricetus auratus – or golden hamster.

He brought the animal back to the United
Kingdom where they were enthusiastically
greeted as pets. But their popularity
wouldn't last.

It appeared that owning a small hamster
was merely a trend – a craze, if you will –
and before you could say "hamster whee "
the rodents disappeared from the landscape
of the nation.

But that wasn't about to end the
importation of this guy into the realm of
domesticated pets. Fast forward to the 20th
century – 1930 to be exact – when another
zoologist, this time Israel Aharoni from
Hebrew university in Jerusalem, discovered
a female hamster complete with twelve
offspring in the Syrian Desert.

Who would think that a discovery like this would rock the zoological world? But indeed it did. For those who took their study of rodents seriously – and professionally – Dr. Aharoni had just delivered quite a coup.

Few professionals – let alone laymen – had even heard of the hamster. Those who had, knew that not one had been spotted in nearly 100 years. The natural assumption among the professionals was that the species had become extinct.

The professionals now learned with this discovery that the animal was merely elusive – preferring to live the life of a hermit, out of view. He actually thrived in the tunnels they created.

Dr. Aharoni did what any respectable zoologist would do – he took the newly discovered family back to Jerusalem with him. Unfortunately, he knew far too little about what was needed to keep them alive. Only a quarter of the litter survived.

But he was able to breed those who did survive. But the road to celebrity status was not to be an easy one for the hamster. And he had to endure some years of hardship.

As you may know, it wasn't very long ago that the hamster was used for the longest time as a laboratory animal. While this may not have been a

HAMSTERFACT: THE TOES!

When you get a chance to examine a dwarf hamster up close and personal, take a good look at his feet. Yes, his feet. In fact, take a good hard look at his toes, to be specific.

The dwarf hamster has four toes (count 'em if you don't believe me!) on his front feet. His back feet though have five toes each. You'll also notice that his feet are pretty darned furry.

humane fate for this tiny creature, his status helped to teach us ultimately how to keep the animals healthy in captivity. And as you might guess, this knowledge would be essential later when he becomes a popular pet.

You can still find an occasional lab hamster, though not nearly as many as a generation ago. Today, he's the revered pet of many a household.

CHAPTER ONE
A BREED APART: TYPES OF DWARFS

So what kind of dwarf hamster do you want? Yes, I understand a small one. That's pretty much a given, you know? What I mean is what species of dwarf hamster do you prefer Chinese? Striped? Perhaps even Campbell's Russian hamster?

Yes, those names are very international sounding. And surprisingly, a variety of different species of these small critters exist. If you're considering adopting one of these as a pet, then you'd probably like to know about all of them, so you can make an intelligent and informed decision.

Actually, when you go to adopt your new pet, you have the choice of four separate species: Campbell's, sometimes called Djungarians, Roborovskiis, Siberians, sometimes referred to as Winter Whites, or Chinese.

You'll notice as we discuss their physical characteristics the similarities between the Siberians and the Campbell's. They, indeed, are very closely related.

THE CHINESE HAMSTER

Let's discuss the **Chinese Hamster** first. His scientific name is Cricetus griseus. If you mistake this guy for a mouse, we'll forgive you. Many people who aren't very familiar with dwarf hamsters make this mistake. And we'll tell you why right now. This is the only dwarf hamster who has a tail.

If you hear people talk about their Striped hamster or their Chinese striped, they're actually referring to this breed. And while we're talking about this species first, let's get one point out of the way right now. Technically, these hamsters are not true dwarf hamsters. But their size is so similar to the dwarf variety that it's customary just to include them into any description of this sort.

The Chinese Hamster has a slender body. As an adult, he'll get no bigger than four inches (or about 10 centimeters). Indeed, this is small – small enough to squeeze his thin body in between the bars of just about any hamster cage.

Before you buy a cage then, consider housing him in an aquarium. This is a much safer choice. You won't have to worry about this nocturnal animal making a "break out" while you're asleep some night.

The natural coloring of the Chinese hamster is called agouti. This describes the coloring in which their hairs are banded with both light and dark colors. They have a black dorsal line (this is the line that runs down their spine) and ivory bellies.

The only other pattern associated with the Chinese hamster is called the Dominant Spot. This is a white coat with patches or spots of a color.

THE ONLY DWARF WITH A TAIL

Chinese hamsters have a hairless tail which is about an inch long. Because of their tail, you may also hear people refer to this species as a rat-like or a mouse-like hamster.

And even though it's a nocturnal creature, you'll discover the Chinese hamster stirs around some during the day. You may experience a few problems socializing your new friend. He's a bit timid by nature, although he is normally a very good-natured fellow. Some hamsters have the bad habit of nipping, this particular species seldom does this.

The tiny size and swiftness translate into a pet that's quick. And this means they may become quite a little difficult to handle – especially for children. So keep this in mind if the hamster is destined to be a children's pet.

Despite their small size, these guys need lots of room to roam. They're active and need the space to help prevent boredom.

And as sweet as they may be to you, if you're housing these guys in an aquarium with other hamsters, you may run into "roommate" problems. As these hamsters age – especially the females – they may become aggressive with the others living with them. You may even discover that you'll have to separate these from the others.

You may want to consider – right from the

start – housing the Chinese hamster separate from the others. While some owners have been known to keep everyone happy in the same "house," you really can't count on this happening!

You'd care for this hamster just like you would any other. A wire cage, as I've mentioned, may not be the best choice of houses for him. And you really want to avoid the cedar or pine wood shavings that you normally associate with a hamster's cage.

It's important, nonetheless, to keep his cage clean to avoid the buildup of an ammonia-like smell from the accumulated urine.

If you have your mind and heart set on getting a Chinese hamster, be prepared to hunt for one. These guys aren't that common and can be difficult to find. In fact, in California, you actually need a permit in order to own one. So you may want to check with your local pet store or vet to discover any restrictions placed on your owning one of this species.

DWARF CAMPBELL'S
RUSSIAN HAMSTER

The species that scientists call the phodopus campbelli, we know better as the dwarf Campbell's Russian hamster or even as the Djungarian hamster. He's called the Campbell's hamster, not because he loves that brand of soup, but because of W.C. Campbell, who immortalized this little guy.

Campbell found him in Russia in the early 1900s and brought him back to the United Kingdom, where it became all the rage for a while to own this pocket pet. But Russia isn't the only country you'll find this species of hamster. You'll also discover it in China and Mongolia. The lifespan of this little guy is only one and half to two years. When fully grown, he'll be no bigger than four inches.

So just like the Chinese hamster, the best housing for this guy is an aquarium. His size makes it all too easy for him to slide between the bars of any cage.

The hair on the back of a dwarf Russian Campbell's hamster is usually gray-brown. They also possess a darker dorsal strip that runs down the center of their backs. As the fur runs down the sides and eventually to their under side, it slowly turns into a creamy color or even white.

Having said that, though, thanks to extensive breeding, you'll liable to find these hamsters in a variety of coat colors as well as various patterns.

Oh yes, one more thing! You may instantly recognize a dwarf Campbell's Russian hamster by his furry feet!

The Campbell's hamster is nocturnal, but you may find that some time throughout the day he stirs around a bit for you. And even though they make great pets, this species has the tendency to nip at you if they feel threatened. And just like the Chinese species, their small size give them the gift of swiftness, which may be a hindrance when you or especially your children are trying to hold them.

Russian Campbell's hamsters are actually quite friendly with each other, unlike the Chinese hamsters. You'll have no problems keeping them all in one cage. (Just be sure that you keep the males away from the females unless you intend to breed them). This is especially true if kept together from an early age. If you plan on introducing a younger member to an older one, they may encounter a few issues.

The basic care of this species is the same as

described for the Chinese hamster.

While Dwarf Winter White Russian Hamster
is his official name, you may hear some
people refer to this variety as the Siberian
hamster or even the Siberian dwarf.
Technically, his species is called the
phodopus sungorus.

This species of the animal usually lives
between one and a half and two years and
grows to be about three and a half inches in
length. It's unusual to find any of this
variety to grow more than four inches. This
makes him a most "compact" pet.

Again, you probably don't want to house
this hamster in a cage; an aquarium would
be a much better choice.

There's a reason why this hamster is called
a Dwarf Winter White Russian hamster.
Normally these animals possess a dark gray
coloring on their backs while the dorsal strip
that runs down their backs is usually black.
The fur on their stomach is normally white.

But, in the winter months, you may
discover that the fur actually turns varying

shades of white. This change in color is actually the result of the change in the length of the number of daylight hours.

But don't be surprised if you find this species in colors other than this as well. Selective breeding techniques have resu ted in several coat colors as well as various patterns. And, winter white Russian hamsters have furred feet.

This nocturnal animal makes a good pet; the average dwarf winter white is generally a naturally good-natured addition to any family. But, again, because of their small size they may be difficult to handle. You may find them squirming right out of your hands – or the hands of your children.

These hamsters are quite sociable in groups. No need to separate them for this reason. But, you do need to make sure that they grow up together. It's not a good habit to introduce an adult to a new baby hamster.

You'll take care of your dwarf winter white species just like you would the Campbell's. Make sure that regardless of the species you choose, you feed him a good quality food that's supplemented with small amount of fresh foods.

The Roborovski hamster belongs to a species whose scientific name is Phodopus roborovskii. This little pet lives to be about three and a half years old, but even among dwarf hamster standards, they're tiny. They grow no larger than two inches in length.

But what they lack in size they make up for in speed. This is the "Speedy Gonzalez" of the dwarf hamster set.

Because of their small size, you can definitely rule out housing them in a cage. They could probably fit through the bars any number of ways. Again, an aquarium would be the best house you can buy for them.

As with all the other hamsters, you'll discover the Roborovski to be most active at night. In fact, this particular specie is noted for rising at dusk and keeping himself busy most of the night.

You'll find that the natural color of the Roborovski hamster is a sandy brown along their backs. Their stomach is normally white. In addition, their coloring includes distinctive white markings over both of their eyes. You may also find a white-faced variety of this species of dwarf hamster.

They are a good natured animal; you'll seldom find one of this kind nipping you. But with tiny size makes them extremely fast and uniquely agile. This means that picking them up to love them when they don't want to can be daunting. And remember if you're having trouble handling this tiny guy, your smaller children will have even more difficulties with him.

In fact, they are so agile, some hamster lovers have discovered – through personal experience, no doubt – that you should make sure you're in an area where finding and catching them would not pose much of a problem. The odds are that great they once you pick them up, they'll get away from you!

Some people even suggest that you only handle the Roborovski over a large box. If they escape your grip then they'll land in the box. And as you may already have guessed, you may want to keep them in a large space – these animals need room to move about (quickly!)

Don't worry about keeping this species in their own individualized housing units. They are social and can easily be kept in groupings or pairs of the same sex (unless you're prepared to deal with the offspring!)

Chapter Two
What To Expect
When You Adopt

J ust looking at your pet hamster can tell you quite a bit about the characteristics of him. First, look at those soulful large eyes. Gorgeous, aren't they?

While the eyes may be the mirror of the soul, in the case of the hamster, it's the mirror of the hours that he keeps. You can tell merely by the large size of the eyes that your hamster is a nocturnal animal. He's an animal that's awake at night and sleeps during the day.

And now wonder. His origins are from the desert, His ancestors – and contemporary cousins – prowl the arid range at night, when the temperatures are cooler. During they day, they sleep (much like your teenage children!)

Next examine the hamster's ears.
Positioned high on the rodent's head, these
ears are indicative of an animal who
possesses a keen sense of hearing. They're
positioned high on the head to take
advantage of that very trait. After all, he
needed this for protection from various
predators in the wild.

Check out those cute whiskers! They're
more than just an attractive appendage.
Whiskers perform a very valuable task.
They're essentially the way that the
hamster touches his world.

That's right! The hamster uses these
whiskers – called vibrissae in the zoological
world – to guide them along. And his face
isn't the only place you can find whiskers.
He also has these valuable tools on the
sides of his body.

The average hamster relies quite heavily on
the whiskers to help him from falling off or
bumping into objects.

And because a hamster's eyesight isn't
remarkably clear, these whiskers help him
during the day as well as at night when he's
tunneling and its virtually impossible to see
because of the dark.

That could very well be the mantra of your pet dwarf hamster. Perhaps he can't see very well, but he's honed his sense of smell quite well, thank you very much.

Hamsters, in fact, depend on their sense of smell to lead to not only food, but water as well (I bet that's something you can't do, find water by smell alone – and chlorinated water doesn't count!)

Their nose also warns them of impending danger. It helps to identify other animals, helps them find their way back home and believe it or not, it also helps to tell them the right time to breed. In more ways than one, a hamster's very survival depends on it sense of smell.

And while we like to credit his nose for his incredible power, the truth of the matter is that the hamster has scent glands on other parts of his body. These scent glands produce a musk-like fluid, which is primarily used to attract the opposite sex. It's also used to mark and identify his territory and quite frankly, to recognize individual hamsters. These are called midventral scent glands.

Some species of hamsters even have a
second set of scent glands located on either
side of their bodies. This particular type of
gland is larger on the male than the female.
It's also influenced by the sex hormones.

You can recognize these glands in the male.
They're the dark pigmented areas on the
side surrounded by dark, bristly hairs. In
the female, the hair around the side glands
are softer. If you can't see them right
away, watch a hamster groom himself. He
spends much time grooming these glands
(can't be too good looking for the opposite
sex, now can you?)

You'll discover more about his incredible
sense of smell later in the book, when we
explain how to orient your new pet to your
presence and his new surroundings!

The scarcity of food in her natural habitat
contributes to another physical trait as well:
the need for speed. When you adopt your
pet dwarf hamster you'll know exactly what
we mean.

You'll discover that your hamster needs
exercise – and plenty of it. The stereotype
of a hamster running on a wheel getting

nowhere, while humorous, is extremely accurate!

In the wild, the hamster needs to travel vast distances (especially in relation to his size) in order to find enough food.

Of course, this physical trait shouldn't be much of a surprise to you. In the desert where food can be hard to come by, storing what you do find for later only makes sense from a survival standpoint.

But, unfortunately, animal behaviorists don't know as much as they would like about the dwarf hamster's wild relatives. Naturally a burrower, the untamed hamster spends much of her time underground. She prefers to hide in the cool recesses of tunnels, far away from the glaring sunlight.

WHAT TO EXPECT
FROM YOUR HAMSTER

If you've never adopted a hamster before, you may have many preconceived ideas about the traits and habits of these furry little creatures. Some of what you've heard, in fact, may be right on target.

Let's take the idea that they're known for their chewing anything in sight. If you believe this about a dwarf hamster, then you're right. And you know what you're getting into should you decide to adopt one.

Saying that hamsters love to chew would be an understatement. These cute little guys even love to chew the bars on the cage. So, rest assured that if your hamster chews incessantly, he's really not obsessive. A genuine physical reason exists for his habit.

He's only trying to trim his teeth. A hamster's teeth never stop growing. Have you ever heard the saying he's 'long in the tooth" when referring to an older person. It may not make sense when talking about people, but it makes perfect sense when you think about the hamster.

In order to keep their teeth at an acceptably reasonable size, they must constantly chew.

But please, don't let him chew on the metal bars of his cage. This according to some experts can damage his brain.

Instead, provide him with plenty of "chewing material." You can buy wooden chews at the pet store. You can also let him chew fruit tree branches.

You've no doubt heard tales of new hamster owners being kept up all night because their pet is busy running on his wheel. So do hamsters really spend that much time running?

HAMSTER:
THE FITNESS EXPERT OF THE RODENT SET

Indeed they do. They enjoy their exercise. An average hamster, in fact, runs about the equivalent of two miles a day. Not bad for a tiny animal that's barely four inches long himself. There's no getting around it; you'll have to include that infamous hamster wheel in his cage.

And along with the need for exercise comes the common complaint among new hamster owners: they choose to run like the wind in the middle of the night. Yes, this is true as well.

Hamsters are nocturnal animals. This means that they're most active at night and sleep during the day (similar to the average American teenager!)

Now, knowing this, we'll give you one piece of advice: Unless you are up half the night you probably shouldn't set up you hamster's cage in your bedroom. In fact, even before you bring your hamster home, think hard about where you do want it to be located.

Similarly, the cage shouldn't be in one of your children's bedroom either – if, that is, you want your child to get any sleep at night.

Instead of trying to curtail your hamster's activity level, you should be encouraging it. Your job, if you want to be a good hamster parent, is to provide your new pet with the practice for the dwarf hamster marathon that he craves.

The Traditional Hamster Wheel

You've seen it movies and in television shows: The proverbial hamster wheel. Yes, these animals really do love to run on it. That's because they need as much exercise as they can get! So, in anticipation of this (and we'll talk in more depth about these wheels later) let's just say you'll want your hamster's cage somewhere in the home in which you won't hear the wheel at 2:30 in the morning.

Don't be too shocked if you discover that your Henry Hamster begins to gnaw at his plastic exercise wheel. Yes, indeed, it just might happen. If it does, please remove as soon as you notice this is occurring. Plastic – even well-chewed plastic – is not the stuff a hamster's diet should be made of.

You'll want to switch to a metal wheel if this happens. And this could cause you some problems. You may have problems finding just the right metal wheel. Most of them, after all, have rungs.

There really are several brands out there that don't have rungs, among them Fern Cage and Quality Cage. These both have solid surfaces suitable for your tiny friend. Both of these companies produce exercise wheels that are basically "gnaw proof."

If you've never bought an exercise wheel for a hamster before, you may not realize that they actually come in varying sizes. You can easily buy a small wheel for your dwarf hamster.

By the way, if you have more than one hamster in the cage, don't expect these creatures to be really considerate. They will not devise a schedule that one hamster can use the cage from 1 a.m. to 3 a.m. and then the other can use if from 3 a.m. to 5 a.m.

Heck, we have a hard enough time getting humans to share, how can we possibly expect hamsters to do this?

No, you know exactly where this is going. Each of your hamsters needs his own cage. Well, let's put it this way, you need as many wheels as you have hamsters. Whether each individual hamster will chose his exclusive "hamster-wheel domain."

Wheel Noise

When you go to the pet store to buy your wheel, let me give you one piece of advice: Check out the noise factor.

Oh, yes, right about now, you may smirk a little thinking this is silly. But when you have to listen to a loud wheel at 3 in the morning, you'll realize that your lack of research may be keeping you up at night!

Don't be shy about asking the pet store clerk to spin that wheel before you buy it. I'm sure you won't be the first customer who has asked to do this.

If you do happen to come home with a squeaky wheel or the wheel you buy develops a squeak after some use, you can try lessening the noise. A little dab of vegetable oil should help.

Indeed, this is possible. Every hamster loves to run – it's part of their genetic make up. But some hamsters have been known to become obsessive about this habit. They'll run themselves to the point of exhaustion.

If you discover this might be just the situation, it's unlikely that your little Henry is running because he's compulsive or he's even training for the New York City hamster marathon. More than likely, he's bored. Or it could very well be that he has no place else to run.

Yes, time's to take a look at the size of his cage again. You may want to give him more room by adding additions, maybe a few more tunnels. Does he have any other "exercise" equipment that he can run on?

Dealing with a bored hamster

If you have children, you've probably heard this lament more than once, "I'm borec!"

So you probably don't want to deal with it from a hamster's point of view. Well, luckily

41

for you then hamsters can't actually talk. But they very well may get bored.

Let's face, it you new pet has every reason to get bored. His house may be gorgeous, but he's literally confined to it for about 23 hours every day. The only time he gets a break to check out new surroundings is when you take him out for his play time. It's no wonder that he may be developing the hamster version of "cabin fever."

So, what's a good hamster parent to do in this situation? Just make sure you provide your pet with enough different activity options as possible. You may want to set up a network of tunnels and mazes to give him more room to roam within the limited amount of space that you have.

Also the various toys can give your hamster a nice, active diversion from running on the wheel.

And finally, does the little guy get his "out-of-cage" experience once a day? Any or all of these alternatives may help you – and Henry – cope with his seemingly compulsive addiction to wheel running.

WHO NEEDS A ZIPLOC BAG
WHEN YOU'VE GOT CHEEK POUCHES?

Are hamsters really like squirrels in that
they store food in their mouth?

Here again, if you've heard this and
believed it, you're absolutely right.
Hamsters are capable of doing this because
they have a pouch in their cheek. He stuffs
these pouches with an immense amount of
food – sometimes food that ways almost
the equivalent of half his body weight.
It's the way they naturally collect and
deliver not only their food, but their nesting
material as well from one location to
another.

To empty his pouch, your hamster uses his
forepaws to push the material or food from
the back of the cheek forward. While it's
not a trait that serves any vital use in a
caged environment, this was of extreme
importance and safety to the feral hamster.

This mechanism allowed them to gather and
keep food through the winter months when
the supplies were hard to find.

HamsterFact: Cheek Pouches

Surprised that your Henry Hamster has cheek
pouches? If you knew the German language,

you might be a little less surprised. The word, hamster, it seems come from the German word, "hamstern" which means to hoard.

The "Out-Of-Cage" Experience

Providing your hamster with an "out-of-cage" experience on a daily basis is essential to his good health and well-being. But, when you do let him "roam free" and enjoy the expanse of a room, you need to ensure that you place him in a safe and secure area. You don't want him running out through the front door.

Hamsters require about one hour of exercise time outside of their cage daily. Not only does this keep them physically fit, but it also stimulates them mentally.

A Family Project?

You wouldn't adopt a dog or a cat without consulting every member of the family, now would you? So why would you even think about bringing home a hamster without talking it over with your spouse and children?

You may have decided that you can live well

with the habits of a hamster, but can everyone in your home? And more importantly, is each member of your family ready to understand – and assume – the responsibilities of ownership of this pet.

Yes, he's small, adorable and appears on the surface to be a low-maintenance choice in pets. But, despite this you – and ideally the rest of your family – have daily obligations to even a four-inch hamster.

Also keep in mind that the very reason why these pets are so adorable is partly why they can be so difficult for some people and especially for youngsters. The size of the hamster provides them with a swift agility. Your pet hamster can squirm and wiggle his way out of your hands quicker than a magician can pull a rabbit out of his hat.

And because of his always growing teeth, the hamster does have a tendency to bite his handlers. This may make many children uncomfortable and as a parent, I can see some strained situations developing.

Is My Hamster Male or Female?

So, you've just bought your first dwarf

hamster. And what's his name?
Henry! Let me see the little guy . . .

Uh! You may want to call your new pet
"Henrietta."

Don't be embarrassed. Lots of people have
a problem distinguishing the sexes of their
dwarf hamster. The real "problem" occurs
because the hamsters themselves have
absolutely no problem telling the boys from
the girls.

Before you know it, if you're not careful,
you can find yourself the proud owners of a
entire family of dwarf hamsters.

So how do you tell the boys from the girls in
the dwarf hamster set? Well, since you're
not one of the species themselves, it may
take a little while. But it's not that difficult.
You can go about it in several different
ways, in fact.

Each of these techniques, by the way, rely
strictly on observation – so they all have
some level of probability built into it.

First, pick up your new pet so you can see
his stomach and his genitalia . . . yes, this
is crucial! You'll know right off if you have a
female, because her stomach will have the

mammary glands – nipples that is for feeding her young. If you can't really tell – and sometimes you can't – there are still several other methods you can use to solve this embarrassing dilemma.

You can always double check this by examining the animal's genitalia. Males of course will have testicles. Then check further – because the animal is so small these methods are sometimes less than foolproof – to see, quite frankly, what some people refer to as "urine holes." Between the vaginal and urinary openings and the anus.

Technically speaking the space between these "urine holes" is called the *anogenital distance.* This specifically refers to the distance between the genital openings and the anus. In the male in the male it would be the distance between the penile opening and the anus. In the females, you're looking at the distance between the vaginal and urinary openings.

 If your new hamster is a male, these orifices are spaced much farther apart (relatively speaking on an animal is four inches long at most!) than the females'.

Of course, eventually you'll get your

"diagnosis" confirmed by a veterinarian, who by the way may have just as much difficulty detected his sex as you!

CHAPTER THREE
ADOPTING YOUR HAMSTER . . .
WITH CARE

This is the big day! Yes, you have all your hamster paraphernalia set up, just waiting for the new arrival. Soon Henry will arrive. Wait! You haven't chosen him yet? You're not quite sure the adoption method you're using?

Don't worry. You've got several options. And you're very smart for setting all of his necessary items up first. That way, when you do bring him (or her) home, you can usher him right into his new castle to start the orientation process. Smart. Very smart.

SO EXACTLY HOW DO YOU ADOPT A HAMSTER?

You've got several options. You can always go to a pet store to adopt one. Pick any pet store in the country. You're bound to find a good supply. Another option, albeit a little less known one, is to adopt a dwarf hamster through a rescue center.

You may even want to visit or call your local animal shelter. This organization may have a dwarf hamster that was brought in. Again, while this is a wonderful thing to do, you don't always know the history of the hamster or how this little guy has been treated.

Adopting Through A Breeder

And then there's the most popular route of selecting a hamster: Through a breeder who specializes in dwarf hamsters. If you're new to hamster ownership, you may want to start with the breeder. After you've owned several hamsters, when you're more experienced with this little guys, you may choose to use a rescue center as an option. But for a novice hamster owner, a rescue-center hamster may come with too many issues for you to adjust to right now.

There are various methods of finding breeders of dwarf hamsters. To locate one close to home, start by checking out the classified section of your local newspaper. You may also want to ask family and friends if they know of any breeders. If they're at all familiar with hamsters, they just might.

The breeder will also help you in choosing the best possible dwarf hamster for your family. If you decide to adopt from a pet store, you may visit the store on the day that the person who is most knowledgeable about the hamsters are off.

But, if you adopt from an individual who has dedicated a certain amount of his time, energy – and, yes, his passion – to the dwarf hamsters, you can feel confident that he's not going to steer you in the wrong direction.

When you adopt from a breeder, you'll also be able to get the exact date of birth of your little dwarf guy. You'll also know more about his parents (and more than likely get to see them too!). You'll know exactly what breeds his parents are as well as how old they are and a little bit about their health history.

As guidelines those, these are some of the qualities you're searching for in your new family member.

First, you want to choose a young dwarf hamster. Now, having said that you don't want to take him from his mom before he's ready. Before you can confidently adopt him, he needs to be at least four weeks old. No younger than that.

If you adopt any hamster younger than this, he just hasn't been weaned from his mother yet. He's still drinking her milk for nutrition. Besides, there are still obviously "hamster traits" he still needs to learn from her. (No, donning that hamster costume and pretending you're his mom is not going to do him any good. And it just may scare the rest of your family.)

You also don't want to adopt a hamster who is older than three month. Preferably you'd like to adopt even before they reach the age of two months. And the reason is simple enough. A female hamster is capable of getting pregnant by the time she reaches her "two-month" birthday. Oh, yes!

If you adopt a female (and you'll recall how tough it is to tell the males from the females when they're that small), you may be adopting in reality an entire litter of

54

dwarf hamsters. Not only that, but a mother hamster that young is probably not a very healthy hamster herself.

Age also is associated with ease in taming the hamsters. The younger a hamster is, the easier the process of orientation. The older the hamster, the longer it'll take for him to get used to you.

Wait till afternoon to select and adopt your hamster. No, this is hamster feng shui in action. It's simple hamster biorhythms at work. Since these animals are nocturnal, the chances are good that if you adopt one in the morning, he's not going to be at his best.

If you wait till afternoon or early evening, then you can see exactly what type of energy level he has and more of his personality can shine through.

PHYSICAL CHARACTERISTICS

Choose a healthy hamster. All right, you say tentatively. How can I tell what a healthy hamster looks like? You can tell easily enough. He'll have clear eyes for starters, he'll be active and he'll have all his fur. If he has some fur loss, it could be because of an underlying health problem.

55

Before you adopt your hamster, check him for bumps or lumps on the body. A healthy hamster has none.

In general, you'll be able to tell a dwarf hamster who is healthy from one that not's so healthy. They'll be a certain glow and vibrancy to him that the one who is struggling with health issues just doesn't have.

I know, all you really sympathetic people out there are telling me those poor less than healthy hamsters need good homes too. And you're right. If you want to work with a less than healthy one from the start, I really can't stop you. But you should have a veterinarian's appointment ready. Take your new friend straight from the place of adoption to the doctor. Get ready to get him healthy!

Seriously consider adopting them in pairs. Hamsters indeed are social animals. This may not be true of the Syrian hamster, who is about twice the size of the dwarf variety. But the little, furry creatures you're considering adding to your home are very social.

Try hard, if you're adopting two, to adopt

two of the same sex. Hamsters cannot be neutered or spayed. (Just how small would those little surgical instruments have to be?) and to suddenly find a litter of hamsters when you awaken one morning would be quite surprising!

Chapter Four
Bringing Baby Home . . .

Before you dash out to adopt your Henry-Henrietta dwarf hamster, you may want to learn a little more about his needs and, most importantly, your role in providing for his needs.

We've already mentioned some his more widely-known habits, so you know what to expect when you bring that bouncing baby dwarf hamster home. But you'll also want to keep him happy as well.

Many people – especially busy parents – believe that they can adopt a hamster for their children instead of going through the traditional dog or cat pet ritual with them. They believe because these animals are small and can function well in a cage that they somehow require less attention than a pet dog or a cat.

If you're considering the adoption of a dwarf hamster based on this logic – I would strongly advise you not to adopt. The truth of the matter that your average dwarf hamster requires as much as, if not more attention, than your traditional pets.

First, the metabolism of this tiny creature demands that he receives plenty of exercise – more exercise than he can get on his own by living in his cage for 24 hours a day, seven days a week.

This means he'll need at least one hour a day of free-roaming time. This is essential and cannot be neglect any more than you can neglect taking your dog outside.

You must also take into consideration that the dwarf hamster is difficult to handle physically. Again, this tiny adorable body makes him a swift and agile creature. He'll "escape" from your arms in a heartbeat. Children – especially very young children – have a difficult if not impossible time holding them. And this only creates a high level of frustration for them.

Hamsters are just like any other animal. Once you bring your new baby home, you'll need some time to establish a bond with him as well as trust. That's why your first month with your new pet is the most important.

Keep in mind that when you bring your hamster home, he is quite frightened. Whatever you do, don't force the poor creature out of the travel box that you brought him home in.

Instead, simply open the box. Allow him to emerge from there in his own time and when he's ready. This makes it essential of course, that you've already established his cage, making it a secure house for him.

Once your hamster has come out of his box (and don't worry, he will!) don't even try playing with it for a while. In fact, according to animal behaviorists, the best approach is to actually leave the cage in the dark for up to five days. This allows your hamster plenty of time to calm down and adjust to the new surroundings. (You'll have plenty of time soon to introduce yourself!)

During these "five days of darkness" you can and should talk to your new pet. But talk to him in a calm, soft voice. Some new hamster owners even read to him. No, he really doesn't care what type of reading material you read out loud. But the act of reading does accustom him to the sound of your voice.

Beginning on the fourth day of the "five days of darkness" – and continuing for several days after that -- introduce him to a tissue with your scent on it. In this way, he can recognize you when you do start interacting with him. You're not so much a stranger.

You should also begin to feed your new pet treats starting the fourth day (healthy treats, of course!) Don't give me that blank stare! Your hamster loves all sorts of "people food". You probably don't realize this yet, but as you become a veteran owner of one of these delightful dwarf hamsters, you'll discover this.

Feeding your hamster healthy treats means giving the little guy (or gal!) sunflower seeds, pumpkin seeds on occasion. But be careful. As healthy as these both are, they are also fattening. And when you're only four inches long, it doesn't take much of a weight gain for it to become noticeable!

Many owners opt to feed their hamsters yogurt drops as treats. But these can be fattening too, as can commercially manufactured treats. It's much better to supply your dwarf hamster with peas and carrots as treats or any other type of vegetable that he may want to eat.

You can try treating your hamster to an occasional piece of fruit, but this category of food should be kept to a minimum. But there's no reason why fruit can't be part of the introductory treats.

THE DWARF HAMSTER WHISPERER

Now that your hamster is calm and adjusted to his new surroundings, literally got a whiff of what you're like and has accepted treats from you, it's time to start the fun part – playing "dwarf hamster whisperer."

Don't laugh! This is exactly what you're doing now. It's time to "tame" your litt e hamster. This process introduces him to you. It's necessary if you ever want to hold or move your newly adopted pet. (And just look how cute and cuddly he is; we know you can't wait to pick him up!)

Start by opening the cage door (slowly, now, you don't want to startle him!) and placing a bit of tissue with your scent in the cage. Then you very slowly put your hand in the cage. Whatever you do, don't wiggle your fingers or try to reach in to pet your hamster yet.

These first steps allow him to recognize that it's your scent on the tissue he's come to accept. Give him a little time to realize that the scents are one and the same!

He'll probably amble over and sniff your fingers. Keep them still. He's doing the hamster "getting-to-know-you" strut. He may even walk over your hand. This is a good thing.

If he bites you try not to react by quickly pulling your hand away. In this case, slowly remove your hand from the cage – and remember to shut the door.

Check out your hand and fingers to ensure that he didn't bite hard enough to draw blood. Wait a few minutes and try this process again. If he bites you again, leave your hand in the cage (as long as he didn't bite hard enough to cause you to bleed.)

If the second time he still bites and you're

bleeding, slowly take your hand out and call it quits for the day. Begin the whole process again tomorrow. And don't get discouraged. Look at the size of you – and your hand – in comparison to him. The poor creature has no other way to communicate right now! Don't take the bite as a personal affront.

This familiarization period, by the way, is a long process. Some owners say that it has taken them up to three months or longer to gain the trust of their pet hamsters. (I told you that these guys need just as much attention as a dog or a cat!)

Whatever you do, don't try to rush your hamster into accepting you. This process just doesn't work like that. In many ways, he's the one in charge of the length of the introductions. Follow his lead and try to be patient in the process. I promise you the rewards are many.

Once your Henry Hamster is adjusted to the presence of your hand, then your next step is an attempt at petting him. But for now, your aim is to only pet him on his back. And never, ever "sneak up" on Henry Hamster from behind. And whatever you do, keep using that scented tissue as an introductory tool that precedes the emergence of your hand in the cage.

Again, getting you and your pet to the point where you can pet him may take some time. So while I'm mentioning this in passing, you may feel as if you're "stuck" at this point for an inordinate amount of time. But, if you're patient, you'll soon discover a wonderfully fulfilling relationship with this pet.

Once he allows you to pet him, your next step is to learn how to move him to his "playpen." Don't move him merely by picking him up. He's still a bit too frightened for this. You may have already bought a "hamster ball" that he likes to roll around in. This is an ideal way to take him to his new play area.

His playpen needn't be elaborate. You may want to pamper him and buy him one from a pet store, but that's not necessary.

His new playground may be as simple as the bathtub. If you choose the bathtub just follow these two simple rules before he jumps in. First, block the drain! And place towels down on the floor of the tub so it doesn't turn into a slip and slide toy for him.

And when I call this a "play" pen, that's exactly what I mean. Make sure you stock this area, whatever you use, with an abundance of "hamster toys". You'll also want to make sure that there's enough room for you to interact with him. You, ideally, will want to sit on the floor with him and play with him.

And here's another hint. Arrange it so that your dwarf hamster has to climb on your hands to get into the new play area.

Realize, too, that this is a huge accomplishment. It may not happen on the first or even second try. So don't get disappointed if you get him to his new area and he refuses to walk on your hands to get there. Simply take him back to his cage. He will come to that point where he'll be more than happy to crawl all over you to get to his playtime.

And when it does occur, allow your hamster to play for about a half an hour. Then it's time to go back "home." Initially, during this time, you're not going to interact with him. Yeah! I know that I told you to make the area large enough that you have room to play with him.

But, the first several trips to the area just

aren't right for this. This is his time to get used to a new area and to get some exercise.

During this time period, even though you're not interacting or playing with your hamster as much as you'd like, you are allowing him to get used to you! He's familiar with your scent; he's crawling over your hand; you're petting him.

You are, in effect, establishing yourself first as a nonthreatening presence in his life. Soon, the time will come when you'll be more than just a "nonthreat". Just be patient.

When you feel that your hamster is ready, you'll approach him in his playpen. This is accomplished the exact same way you did when he was in his cage.

While he's in his playpen, you introduce him to your scented tissue and hold your hand still for him to investigate. You do this as often as you need to until he doesn't bite you. Trust me, you'll know (especially now that you've been through this process once) when it's time to move on to the next level of contact.

Go through the entire process as slowly or

as quickly as your hamster allows. You'll want to eventually be able to pet his back while he's in his play area.

Once your hamster interacts with you on every level he has done in his cage, it's time to let him run from your left hand to your right and back again. Yep, just let him roam around on you. He may even want to run across your arms. Let him! You two are well on your way to a great relationship! Congratulations.

HOLDING YOUR HAMSTER

Yes, you can do this! And it's much easier than you think. Oh, I know I've warned you about the agility and swiftness of this little guy. And indeed, he's everything I've said he is. But, he's anything but impossible to keep in your hands, as long as you know a few little tricks.

Before we go any further there's something very important you must know about your hamster. Well, about all dwarf hamsters as it turns out. Everyone of them is near-sighted. That's right. They all have a very limited view of the world.

Knowing this dictates in large degree how to approach this small, furry animal. Only handle your hamster when you're sitting down. And always allow your friend to smell and actually see your hands before you pick him up.

Then once you do have him in your hands, hold him firmly there. Don't allow him to squirm or jump out of your hands. The best method for this is to cup both of your hands around the animal, leaving only a tiny hole for him to poke his head through. In this way, you have a good, firm grasp on him, but he can still see what's happening around him.

And since your hands are cupped around him, he should feel pretty safe as well. But be careful with this technique. It's far too easy to squeeze that little guy too hard. So make sure that you leave enough room between your hands. After a few trial rounds you'll know exactly how to do it.

You can also use this method when you carry the hamster across the room or when you pick him up from the ground. Once you get used to holding him, allow him to run from one hand to another. Even let him run across your arms.

Now that you've mastered the "two-handed-cupped approach" to handling your new friend, you're ready to try another technique. Try picking up your hamster using only one hand.

Carefully – and only after your pet has smelled you and seen your hand – curl your fingers around his cute, little body. Now gently lift him, bearing in mind not to squeeze him. Especially be careful not to squeeze him below his forelegs. He'll have one heck of a time breathing if you do this.

This is great method if you plan to carry him only short distances. But it's not a safe or secure method if you plan on carrying him for any length of time or for long distances.

THE SCRUFF METHOD

There is one other method of handling your dwarf hamster. But it should be attempted only by an individual who is an experienced animal handling and is especially skilled in handling dwarf hamsters.

You may hold him from the scruff of its

neck, much like you see animal mothers pick up their children and carry them around. When you hold an animal in this fashion he immediately becomes still.

Again, only those who know how to use this procedure should pick up a dwarf hamster this way.

What does a dwarf hamster eat, anyway?

For the most part, you can feed your new pet a good hamster food seed mixture. You can find these at just about any pet stores. Given his tiny little body, he only needs to be fed once a day. And believe it or not, two tablespoons of this mixture a day should suffice nicely. You should feed him in the early evening, just as he's waking up to start his day.

You should also consider supplementing this little guy's diet with a regular mixture of fresh greens. These could be lettuce, raw green beans. Don't overfeed him though.

And here's a quick note right at the outset. Dwarf hamsters are prone to developing diabetes. So if you must feed your hamster a food that is relatively high in sugar content, do so sparingly.

If you give him these types of food, give him just enough for him to eat in about 20 minutes. If there are "greens" left over, then remove them from your hamster's cage.

You need to be careful about this diet. If you notice that he's having more bowel movements than normal after you feed him this food, then go at least two days without feeding him this diet. Then gradually re-introduce the "greens" diet every other day for the next 10 days. During this period, be sure to see how his system is handling this.

If it all possible, avoid drastic changes in your pet's diet. If you must change his food, then introduce it to him a little at a time. The best method is to mix it slowly with the current food he's eating.

Over the next two weeks, you can gradually increase the ratio of new food to his current food.

Are there any foods that I shouldn't be feeding my hamster? Well, as a matter of fact, there certainly are!

HamsterFact: Coprophagy

This is as good as time as any to introduce you

to the practice of coprophagy. When stated like this, it sounds very important. But what it really means is that your new pet dwarf hamster may eat his own feces.

And you needn't worry about it! Hamsters are one of the few animals (guinea pigs and rabbits do this too!) that eat their nutrient-rich feces. Not only that, it's apparently good for them. It enriches their diet with valuable B vitamins.

Hamsters actually produce two distinct types of feces. The variety that is vitamin-rich and they eat is formed in a section of their system called the blind gut. This feces is smaller than the other and darker. Additionally it's also a little softer than the second kind of feces.

These droppings are also eaten directly from the feces, so anything you find in the cage, that has already been expelled from your pet can safely be cleaned.

Generally speaking, hamsters are willing to eat just about anything. So, just because you put a specific type of food in his cage and he gobbles it, doesn't necessarily mean it's good for him. Hamsters have been known to eat everything from collard greens to lean meat and fish.

In fact, the only restriction on their diet is what you decide to put in their food bowls. So choose carefully. But, it may be a very good idea to stick close to a commercially mixed food. These foods are more likely to provide your hamster with the required proteins, minerals, vitamins and other nutrients your pet needs in the proper ratio.

The other foods – the "greens" diet and other "human" food – should only be fed to the dwarf hamster as a supplement to augment his diet and provide him with some variety.

Of course, this should go without saying, but you should never, *ever* give your dwarf hamster any type of alcoholic beverage. This is the surest and swiftest way to kill the animal.

Don't even think about giving him just "a couple of drops" of these beverages as a "joke." Just look at his size. Even a couple of drops of alcohol can kill him.

IN A PICKLE WITH PICKLES

Another food that you must never, *ever* give your dwarf hamster is a pickle. Don't even think about giving your female pregnant dwarf hamster a pickle (regardless of how much she begs for one!). The pickle, just like alcohol, is a killer of the dwarf hamster.

And while we're talking pickles, you should feed your hamster any type of food that has a vinegar based. It's deadly to these animals.

As tempted as you might be, don't "treat" your new pet to any type of gum, gumball, toffee or caramel. Steer clear of feeding him, in fact, any type of sticky candy. The problem with this type of candy is that it can stick inside the pouch of the hamster, causing him to drool. But more than that, this type of candy may also stick in his very small throat. And he may suffocate.

Hard candy is also a food you should avoid giving your hamster. That means you shouldn't be feeding your hamster lollipops, hot fireballs, sourballs, or any other candy along those lines.

Again, these can all too easily get caught and stuck in your pet's throat. They can cause suffocation far too easily.

You shouldn't feed your hamster food that has already been touched by other animals. Now this may sound a bit strange, but there's really a very good reason for this.

The possibility exists that the food could have been urinated on by the animals, and this could potentially poison your pet.

Also don't feed your new pet any foods which have been left uncovered. It could have bacteria on it. Given the tiny size of a dwarf hamster, it doesn't take a lot of bacteria to make a dwarf hamster sick.

You probably don't want your hamster to eat cheese either. While it won't kill, poison or even make him sick, it very well may make you sick. His eating cheese causes his bowel movements to stink. And you'll end up cleaning his cage more often than you care to!

Don't feed him citrus fruits. Okay, I know that dwarf hamsters just love all fruits and vegetables. But those fruits from the citrus family should not be fed to that cute little guy. They contain citric acid, which could make him very ill.

And if it's food specially tailored for the digestive system and nutritional needs of another animal, please don't be tempted to feed this to him either.

Many people, for example, think – for some

reason – that dwarf hamsters can eat the commercially manufactured food made for rabbits. Rabbits need less protein, so this really doesn't help your little guy at all.

Some pet foods contain specific ingredients that are solely intended for that certain animal. If you feed these foods to your new friend, it may hurt him.

WHAT ABOUT WATER?

Of course, every animal needs water, but perhaps none so much as your dwarf hamster. Make sure your hamster has access to a bowl of water every day. If you know you have trouble remembering to change the water every day, you can purchase a small animal water bottle.

These are available at just about every pet store. They are large enough to hold about a week's supply of water for a dwarf hamster. This means you only have to remember to change the water on a weekly basis.

If you do decide to buy one of these, the tip should be metal and not plastic. If it's plastic, your hamster will chew and destroy it. These could be bad on two levels. First, he's destroyed a perfectly good water bottle. You'll have to go buy another one.

But secondly, by damaging the tip, he's probably also caused a flood in his cage.

If you decide to use a bowl and the not water bottle, buy a rather sturdy, heavy one. Your new pet, in his exuberance at playing, may accidentally knock it over sometime during the night. If this occurs while you're sleeping, then he won't have any liquids.

Taking Care of Your Hamster
In a Nutshell

Below is a quick wrap up of daily tasks that need to be done to ensure your hamster stays healthy and happy. You can print it out if you'd like to stick on your refrigerator door to remind your family of what needs to be done. It also is useful in judging whether you have the time for a hamster in your life right now.

DAILY DUTIES

1.   Check in with your hamster. Look at his physical traits. Does he look healthy? If his eyes are dull, or he appears to be acting under the

weather, determine whether you need to make an appointment with your veterinarian.

2.   Empty the food bowl of uneaten food. Replace it with fresh food.

3.   Change the water in the water bottles.

4.   Remove any soiled or wet bedding.

5.   If he has a litter box, check the box.

6.   Hold your hamster friend daily.

7.   Provide him with his "out-of-cage" experience!

Weekly Tasks

The following tasks should be performed once a week.

1.   Change the bedding in the hamster's cage.

2.   Clean out the water bottles (in addition to just changing water).

3.   Examine your hamster friend
       carefully to ensure no physical
       problems exist. Make sure he hasn't
       cut himself anywhere or any bald
       spots.

4.   Look over your supply of food for
       your pet. Make sure you're not going
       to run out unexpectantly. If you're
       low, put it on your shopping list.

5.   Clean any "cruising" tubes in the
cage.

6.   Make sure the area around the cage
is clean.

MONTHLY CHORES

And yes, there are some aspects of hamster
care that you'll need to perform once a
month as well.

1.   Wash the cage. You'll want to use a
       mild detergent or a deodorizer. Allow
       the cage to soak for a few minutes.
       Then wipe it down with a washcloth.
       Allow it to dry completely.

2. Thoroughly wash out all food bowls,
water bottles and toys.

How would you like to be the first "kid" on the block with a trained dwarf hamster? That's right! I'm talking about a hamster that will perform tricks at your command.

Sound impossible? Well, really it isn't. And it isn't that difficult. So whatcha say? Are you in? Great.

First, you've got to be sure that your dwarf hamster is thoroughly trained. Once you're sure of that, there's really nothing that can get in your way. Your first step is to stock up on some sunflower seeds. This is your hamster's reward for performing these tricks.

And the first one we're going to teach him is to "stand pretty." No, I don't mean sit pretty. A dog may be able to sit pretty. This little creature can "stand pretty."

Take a sunflower seed. Hold it above your hamster's head, much like you were offering a dog a treat and making him . . . well, sit pretty! You hamster will stand on his hand legs in order to reach this treat. When he does this say the words, "sit pretty."

Practice this several times throughout the day with your pet until he "stands pretty" even when you're not holding the treat. After a bit of practice and patience, your dwarf hamster will stand elegantly upon command . . . at least as elegantly as all four inches or so of him can.

"POTTY-TRAINING" YOUR HAMSTER

Yes! It really is possible. Hey, if people can teach their cats to use the toilet and not the litter box, why can't you teach your hamster to urinate in a bottle?

Again, all that's really required on your part is patience . . .and well . . . a bottle. Your bottle needs to be large enough that your hamster can turn around in it. For most dwarf hamsters, a one-pint wide mouth jar works perfectly (think canning jar here!) Place this jar on its side in the section of the cage your hamster as already designated as his bathroom (why buck tradition?).

If you think it's necessary you could place some of his droppings in the jar so he gets the idea of what exactly the jar is for. This though technically isn't necessary.

Make sure your hamster sees you place the jar in this spot. This way you know that he knows that it's there.

If you can't find a bottle that you would consider a suitable size, visit your local pet store. Some stores have actually started stocking hamster potties. And these devices are quite reasonably priced.

Yes, They Do Make Hamster Litter Boxes

Some designs are triangular, created to fit snuggly into a corner of the cage. Others are rectangular. But they all have either a hinged or a removable top. And of course, they all have an opening in the front that' s just the right size for your hamster's convenience.

What would a hamster litter box be, by the way, if it had no litter in it? And this too you can buy at your nearest pet shop. When you buy the litter box, more than likely the kit comes with your first bag of hamster litter.

But even at their tiny size, this bag of litter

just doesn't last forever. Some hamster owners decide that what's good for a cat is good for a hamster. They purchase clumping cat litter to place in the box.

And this isn't all together a bad choice. After all, it's economical, dust-free, and s easy to clean. Just make sure if you go this route that you also buy the scent free variety.

Many owners are fearful of cat litter – and for good reason. Most of the brands on the market today contain silica dust. And this very well could injure your precious little hamster.

If you can find something called "clumping wheat", this is a far better choice. But, just like with the cat litter, be sure that you purchase one of the "new, improved" varieties on the market that are dust free.

But wait, don't run off just yet to buy this. I've got a couple more options you may want to try.

Clumping corncob. Okay, so it sounds a little crazy, but it does work. The only problem may be that your hamster doesn't like the scent.

If all else fails, you can try using a pelleted litter. This is normally made from wood, paper, and either grain or grass. These pellets, though, have a distinct disadvantage. It's extremely difficult to judge the soiled pellets from the fresh pellets.

But in just about every other way, the pellets do a great job of acting as hamster litter. They are super absorbent and control the order amazingly well.

And you don't need to scoop these things out. Every couple of days, you just toss them out and fill the hamster litter box with fresh. What could be easier?

BEDDING MATERIAL
AS LITTER

Many hamster owners prefer to use bedding material as litter. And this is fine too. Actually, it's what your hamster would be using if you didn't provide him with a litter box.

But . . . and here's the catch . . . if you do, then you must clean the litter box on a daily basis. When shavings get wet, they stay wet – and they're smell as well.

The only other word of caution when it comes to litter, is simply this: Keep on eye on Henry the Hamster. These little guys have been known to either eat their litter or to hide it in their cheek pouches.

Some forms of litter can actually damage the pouches. And other litters are just downright dangerous for Henry to be putting in his pouch.

And yes, that's just about the sum total of how that potty training works. The following day you'll more than likely find that he has used it for his toilet.

It's much easier to take the jar and clean his urine from that than cleaning the shavings out of the bathroom corner. Who know that a dwarf hamster could be so cooperative in this way?

Okay, maybe your hamster isn't quite so cooperative. It's altogether possible. While some individual hamsters welcome the bathroom as the ideal addition to their new home, some simply don't get with the program.

They look at this nice little niche in the hamster apartment and . . . well . . . let's just say they get that uncontrollable spark of interior design creativity.

What do I mean by that? Some hamsters won't see the bathroom as a bathroom. Instead, they see it as a kitchen, or a pantry to store their food, or even as an additional private bedroom where they can snuggle and sleep peacefully.

If you discover that your hamster is hoarding his food in his litter box instead of using it for his intended purpose, then his apartment is probably too small for him.

EXTREME MAKEOVER:
THE HAMSTER HOME EDITION

You can probably do it on your own, simply by making a few adjustments.

First, you need to take a good, long, hard look at his cage. Now answer the following question honestly: Is it really big enough for the litter box, his exercise equipment and at least one comfortable sleeping space and still have room for a couple areas reserved strictly for food caches?

Yes, he guy may be small, but he has some serious needs. Remember his ancestors lived primarily underground in tunnels. Based on these needs, it's a safe bet to say that every tunnel had a particular use.

It could very well be that your cage is too small for your pet. Now, you have two options, depending on the type of cage you have. You can either buy a larger cage – which may get expensive, but your hamster will simply adore.

Or you can choose the second option, adding on some sections. If you bought a cage that can accommodate additions, then this just might be the route you want to travel.

What if though the size of the cage isn't the problem? Why then isn't your hamster using his litter box for the intended purpose?

Perhaps Henry the Hamster's sleep box isn't the right size for him. Or maybe he just needs a second one to use as an alternative. It's also possible that he doesn't really care for the nesting material you choose for him.

Oh, I see he urinates in his new litter box, but fails to defecate in it. Believe it or not, this is a common problem. I hate to admit it, but your hamster just may win this battle.

There's not much you can do to force a hamster to defecate inside the box, especially when he's using it for his urine. The only way to really handle this situation is to shrug your shoulders and just clean the droppings.

After all, they are easy enough to clean. All you need to do is to pick them out with an old spoon or a pair of tweezers.

The other problem some owners have is that their hamsters believe that he has more than one bathroom area. He in fact uses two or more corners for his "bathroom breaks". This is a problem for those owners who have provided their hamsters with plenty of room.

Yes, you very well could attempt to train him to use one corner and one corner only. But, it could be just a little too stressful for him. The solution? Start placing litter boxes where ever he decides his bathroom should be. After all, it's really his home!

CHAPTER FIVE
CARING FOR YOUR HAMSTER

He's small. But he has a high metabolism. And that means your Henry Hamster has lots of energy to burn. And there's only two good ways to do this: by having that "out-of-cage" experience we talked about. And enjoying some hamster toys during that experience.

Not only will playing with toys help him with burning his natural energy, but he'll also be able to stay in top physical form – ready for Henrietta Hamster should she arrive anytime soon.

All kidding aside, toys are an important aspect of a hamster's life. It allows him to expend energy and to exercise his muscles.

But then you – as the good hamster parent – are left with two burning questions of the day . . . just what types of toys do hamsters use? And what's the best time of the day to give Henry his "out-of-cage" experience.

Let's answer the second question first. His free roaming playtime needs to be set an hour when it's most useful for him. Waking him from a sound sleep at 3 p.m. because that's the only time you can pencil him into your schedule is not a good idea.

You're only creating the beginnings of mistrust on his part about you. And you're very possibly asking for a nip or two from the little guy.

The ideal playtime for him is the evening, when he's the most alert and energetic. Before you establish a set-in-stone playtime, critically look at the hours he's adopted for sleeping, the hours he's most awake as well as the times of the day (or night perhaps!) that he seems to have the most energy.

Then you can use this time as his playtime. He'll enjoy this time and his health will benefit from using his peak hours for this work out.

But as you have probably guessed by now, it does you little good just to let your furry friend run loose in a room. He needs something to play with. And what he'll love most is to do that things that come naturally to hamster.

In the wild, hamsters cover a minimum of five miles a night rummaging for food. The hamster wheel or bubble ball is a perfect substitute for this activity.

When purchasing a wheel though, be sure to buy either the solid metal version or the all plastic type. You want to avoid buying the wheel that has the rungs. He feet and tail can easily get caught in these rungs and injure your little friend.

Part of his play time includes the ever present habit of gnawing or chewing. As we've stated before, every hamster does this. And not because he's bored. Hamsters continually chew because their teeth continually grow. Hamsters don't have teeth like the human, which emerge from above the gum line and only grow to a certain size, Their teeth continue to grow longer. Chewing is their way of making sure the teeth don't get too long for their mouth.

For gnawing purposes, provide your friend with a twig or a branch. Just be sure it's not been treated with pesticide or other chemicals.

You may also want to place some chewing toys specifically designed for hamsters in his cage as well. Your local pet store has a nice array (probably far too many!) from which to choose. Your hamster will certainly thank you for this.

HamsterFact: Electrical wires

Look around your house. Just about every room has some electric appliance, lamp or other gadget that runs on electricity.

Now take a good look at the floor of these rooms. Are there electrical wires running along the walls? If your house is like most of ours, your answer is a resounding yes.

And here's a hidden danger for your pet hamster. We hardly notice these wires anymore, they're so much a part of our lives. However, your hamster will notice them – without a doubt! In fact, they may be the first items he investigates when you give him his out of cage experience.

To ensure his safety, make sure, before you set him down for his playtime, that all electrical wires are out of his reach. You really don't want him chewing on these!

Let's talk about some of the really cool stuff you can buy for you . . . uhm, your hamster . . . to play with. You may want to buy a toy called a Hamtrac and Ball. It's a plastic ball in which you place your dwarf hamster. You've probably seen this. He can run around without you needed to worry about him chewing any electrical cords or other hazardous objects.

But in addition to that this particular toy also comes with a "track" on which the ball neatly rests. Henry Hamster can run in the ball on the track. And now you don't even have to worry about him taking a tumble down the stairs.

You may still wan to supervise him, however. Some individuals who have bought this toy say that it's just slightly too large for their dwarf hamsters. Some have complained that the toy is too heavy for their pet to navigate around some corners. They just get stuck.

Many people buy it to help their hamsters train for (yeah, this may sound strange if you've never owned a hamster before) "hamster races." And these seem to work well for those "in training."

You may just want to purchase a hamster

ball without the track. If for no other time, the ball comes in handy when you're cleaning the cage. You can place your hamster in the ball, allowing him to run, while you clean the cage.

Who said you need to buy toys?

Oh yes. If you have children, then you are familiar with this parent lament: I spend money on toys and the kids play with the boxes. And so it's the case for your hamster. He'll be delighted to play with anything. Just be sure anything you allow him to use is nontoxic. Remember his system is so much smaller than other animals that he's more sensitive to these things.

For starters, empty toilet paper rolls are great. Your hamster will enjoy this – guaranteed!—and it's just something you were going to throw away anyway.

If you want to provide your pet with a tube for climbing, try creating one out of plastic water bottles. Cut the bottles very evenly. Stick one slightly inside of the other. Now tape them together tightly. And the great aspect of this is you can continue to add to this tunnel any time you like.

Then there's the incredible egg carton. Take the carton your last dozen of eggs came in. Cut the bottom of each indentation where the eggs were placed. Now you have twelve separate holes. Stuff the carton with bedding. Now turn it upside. Allow your hamster to investigate it. He can use it to run around in. Or he may decide it's the perfect place to nest!

After the playing is done

Hamsters, in their native habitat, enjoy spending time curled up in private. They choose places that are hidden from view from just about everybody. It's here that they spend their time both nesting and napping.

You can easily replicate this in his cage by providing him with an empty flowerpot or a wooden box. You'll discover that after a good work out he may head straight for his nesting and napping places for some solitary time.

You'll soon learn that he may also like to hide in "tunnels". In this case, you can provide him with some PVC pipe round enough for him to curl up and nest in.

Let me say right up front: Don't get stressed out about this. Basically under normal circumstances bathing a dwarf hamster is unnecessary. If your hamster isn't sleeping, he'll be running around playing. If he's not running around playing, he'll be gnawing at something. And if he's not gnawing at something . . . he'll be grooming himself.

That's just a long winded way of saying that dwarf hamsters spend time – and lots of it – grooming themselves. In fact, they're like cats in this respect. You'll discover that he'll be fastidious about his hygiene "from paw to tail."

The hamster's original habitat was the desert. So water is very much a foreign object to them. And sticking them in water . . . soaking them to their skin . . . would shock their systems.

And it could give him a chill in the process.

But more than that, excessive bathing can literally strip away the natural oils that are essential to your hamster's healthy skin and fur.

Instead of insisting he take a water bath, try allowing him to give himself a sand bath. Offer your little desert friend a dish of chinchilla sand. You can get these at any pet store. Then watch him roll around, enjoying himself immensely in the process.

Okay, so there may be times when you consider that a water bath may be necessary like . . . ugh! What's that smell?

Well, before you assume that the smell is coming from your pet, investigate his house first. Perhaps there's something you've missed cleaning that needs to be gotten out of his cage.

Go through his entire house. Change the bedding (again if you have to, yes!) with an eye to anything that may be causing this smell. If you've been particularly busy, perhaps you just forgot to change the bedding one day. Or you assigned the chore to another member of the family who failed to understand the importance of keeping the cage clean.

When you make your "housekeeping sweep", look for, in addition to the soiled bedding, any food that may have discarded that he has foraged away. This happens.

Usually, this takes care of the smell. On the off chance that it doesn't though, it could very well be that your hamster isn't feeling well. Now it's time to give Henry Hamster a thorough examination. You're looking for any indication at all that he may not be feeling his perky, energetic self.

We cover the characteristics of a healthy hamster in another chapter. Check out what you should be looking for. If your hamster is feeling a little under the weather, call your veterinarian to schedule an appointment.

Oh, no! You've found the problem! Henry Hamster has gotten himself into some substance (boy we really aren't sure what it is – or was?) that he never should have found.

While we don't know how he managed this, we do know we need to get him cleaned. Just how do we do this? It depends on just what the "something" is.

If your hamster has gotten himself smack dab in the middle of some toxic substance then the most effective way to deal with it is to cut it out of his fur.

Yes. Take a pair of very small scissors –

nail-trimming scissors work well for this –
and cut out, very gently, the affected patch
of fur.

Depending the nature of the substance that,
you may want to just use a soapy washcloth
soaked in lukewarm water to wipe it off his
fur.

We've talked about hamster's teeth. They grow longer for the life of your little friend, that's why one of his hobbies is gnawing. But as with any animal with nails, the time may come when you need to clip his cute little toenails because these grow as well.

You may hold him, wondering just how you trim something this small. Start by buying a pair of nail clippers for babies. Yes, these are just about the tiniest pair you can buy.

Only clip the very ends of the nails. If you've ever tried clipping the nails of a dog or cat, then you realize that holding the animal and clipping the nail at the same time can be nerve racking.

If you're worried about this with your little guy, have someone else hold him while you clip (or if you're just plain "chicken," assign someone else to clip while you hold him.).

If you can't get bear to do this, there is a "cheater's option" that many hamster owners use. That's to line his exercise wheel with a very fine grade of sandpaper. His nails will naturally file down while he runs!

A third option exists (which I personally think is pretty nifty!) and that's hamster wet wipes. Yes, these are wet wipes like you get when you eat barbecue or other messy foods at a restaurant, specially formulated for your hamster. Talk about niche marketing!

You can safely clean – and moisturize, by the way – your baby's coat knowing you're not placing him in any more danger than he's obviously been placing himself in.

If all of these methods of cleaning have failed – and yes sometimes they do – then your veterinarian who'll either have some creative idea or will ask you to bring him in.

Hamster Supply Checklist

The following is a list of the necessities that should already be in place when you bring Henry Hamster home with you on that first day. You may want to print this out so you can take it to the store. You don't want to forget anything important that would cause Henry – or you – any undue stress.

- **Cage**

- **Bedding**

- **Water bottle**

- **Food bowls**

- **Chew sticks**

- **Food**

Now, that you're learning more about your dwarf hamster, you may want to take her to a hamster show. No, it's not a movie theatre just for these cute little rodents. A hamster show is a competitive showing of your pet, just like you'd take a dog to a dog show.

No, I'm not kidding you. Many serious breeders do the "hamster circuit" taking their "pedigreed" friends to these competitions hoping to earn fame and fortune.

If you eventually breed dwarf hamsters, you may want to do the same. More often than not, these competitions are sponsored by local or state hamster clubs. The shows themselves may be held independently, or as part of a larger event venue.

They may even e part of exhibitions that involve other rodents, like rats and mice.

Sometimes you'll find these exhibitions as part of events sponsored by country or state fairs as well.

Whoever sponsors them, you can be sure of one thing: they are pretty much run like any other animal competition. When you visit one of these events, you'll find certain classes for the hamsters, like for color and for color varieties.

The winners of these then are able to take the next step into a more competitive situation until finally there is only one hamster left standing: Best in Show.

HOW DOES THIS ALL WORK?

All of the hamsters are usually displayed anonymously, each in his own show cage. The animals are then judged on their color, structure, hair quality and temperament.

These events are usually reserved for serious breeders, but if you're interested – and not yet a serious breeder – it would be great experience for you to visit a hamster show to get a feel for the competition. It's also a great way to meet breeders if you're having difficulty finding a breeder from whom you can adopt.

CHAPTER SIX
MAKING A CAGE A HOME

When you go to purchase your pet's new home keep one word in mind: Noah. Noah, you ask. Yep. You need to bear in mind, even before you buy his cage, that dwarf hamsters really prefer to live in pairs – just like Noah led his animals to the ark.

This will definitely influence not only what type of cage you'll eventually get for him – or them – but how large it'll be as well.

Let's start by thinking aquarium. A ten-gallon aquarium, with a mesh cover over it may make the best home of all for your new pet. It's cozy for your pet, easy for you to clean and just about every species of hamster likes it.

Not only that, but an aquarium provides you with a very clear view of your new hamster friend. A ten-gallon aquarium can hold about four dwarf hamsters comfortably.

And your budget will like it to. It's relatively inexpensive. But don't forget you'll need to buy a mesh cover as well. the aquarium itself should cost you approximately $10. Remember you don't have to buy all the fish paraphernalia that usually accompanies an aquarium. (You'll be spending that money later for some really cute dwarf hamster toys!)

But before you decide on that, look over the wire cages as well. If you see one of these that you think your hamster will love, just make sure that the bars are spaced close enough together that you won't have to deal with a "break out." Dwarf hamsters are indeed small and agile.

The advantage of a wire cage is that it's naturally well-ventilated. It's also sturdy by design and lightweight. But that same "well-ventilated" advantage can also turn into a disadvantage because these cages also tend to be rather drafty.

Don't take that last remark too lightly either. More than one dwarf hamster has developed pneumonia because of a drafty cage.

The other issue with a wire cage is the hamster's habit of kicking the bedding out of the cage (is this the equivalent, I wonder of your spouse stealing your covers at night?). Your hamster friend will – guaranteed! Just push that bedding that you so lovingly placed in his cage push it all around and right out between the bars in the cage.

And if you're going with the wire cage, make sure that the floor or the bottom of the cage is plastic. If the bottom of the cage is also wire, your little friends may hurt their feet on it. You'll also find a plastic bottom much easier to clean.

This type of cage is also relatively inexpensive, costing anywhere between $12 and $20.

THE HAMSTER CONDO

Then there are those all plastic cages that come complete with tubes, tunnels and hideaways – the condos and playgrounds of happy hamsters everywhere.

This type of cage costs more and is, by the way, just a bit harder to clean. In fact, a penthouse home like this costs a minimum of $30. Depending on size you can spend lots more than that – even upwards of $150. Oh, but your hamster friends certainly will love it!

You can find this type of housing at just about any pet store. More often than not, these elaborate houses are called "Habitrails." You've probably seen them. It's really not uncommon for them to have several floors – at least two and sometimes more. These provide the ultimate living space for your new little furry friends.

Your dwarf hamster may experience some trouble in climbing the tubes, but you can help him out by placing a thin tree branch in the tubes for him to climb.

Now that you've chosen the perfect hamster house, you need to decide where you're going to keep it. Think twice – or even three times – before you make your final decision. Your first concern is to place the new home away from any direct sunlight as well as from any drafts.
You'll also want to make sure that the hamster home is not placed too close to traffic or noise.

And here's where you need to keep another

important piece of information upper most in your mind. Your hamster is nocturnal – he's at his peak level of activity during the night when you're trying to sleep.

Setting up his home in your bedroom – or that of your children's – may not be a good idea.

YOUR HAMSTER'S NEW HOME:
HERE'S WHAT TO LOOK FOR!

Remember the last time you chose a new place to live, whether it was buying a new home or just renting an apartment. It was a big deal. After all, it's where you spend a great deal of your life.

And so it is with your hamster. And unless you find your dwarf hamster a job (Is there a monster.com web site where hamsters can look for work?), he spends even more time in his house than you spend in yours. So, choosing a home for your friend, Henry Hamster is no small decision.

Here are some points to keep in mind when you're out looking at "hamster real estate."

SIZE

Before you buy your home, you should know with some certainty how many dwarf hamsters you're adopting. Then you'll have some idea of the size of the cage. Allow for 20 square inches of floor space –minimum – for every one hamster who'll be living in the home.

If eventually you believe you even may want to breed hamsters, then you need to take this into consideration at the very beginning of your new house search. You may need even a bigger cage for this purpose.

The cage needs to be large enough for the hamsters to maintain their private spaces – and especially a private area for a pregnant or nursing hamster mom.

If your hamster mom feels that any of the other hamsters are threatening her "brood", she may attack them. Or because of the stress she's under due to what she feels like are crowded conditions, she may eat her young.

THINK ABOUT THE SAFETY OF YOUR HAMSTER

If you have other pets in the house – you know, the run-of-the-mill cat or dog –

114

then you should really be very careful if you purchase a cage with bars. The odds are that one of these days your hamster buddies will make a "break for it," simply by slipping through the bars on the cage (And for crying out loud, don't let them watch The Shawshank Redemption, you'll have an escape in no time!)

The Hamster House addition

Every home eventually gets an addition; the hamster home is no exception. Some cages, by their very nature, are designed to facilitate future expansion. This is a good thing.

Usually these types of cages are on the upper end of the hamster real estate market. While this is nice, it really isn't necessary. And it is quite expensive. Unless you have the money to make this kind of upfront investment in Henry Hamster, you probably don't need to worry about that yet.

Making a house a home

And trust me, once your hamster adjusts himself to his new surroundings, he'll waste no time making his new house a well-loved home. Your first task is to line the bottom of the cage with some material that he'll find comfortable.

The type of bedding you purchase for your new pet depends in large part on the type of home you've selected. If you bought a wire or a glass hamster home, then your friend needs some cozy bedding. This bedding is vital to your hamster's happiness. He's about to use it for one of his all-time favorite pastimes, digging and tunneling.

Animal experts recommend that the bedding is composed of aspen shavings, shredded paper or pelleted bedding that's widely available at just about any pet store.

You may think that you should be choosing cedar or pine shavings. But, these particular types of wood shavings create fumes which may irritate your hamster's throat, lungs and nasal passages.

Once you have the bedding, you'll need to create "areas" within the home. You know, you'll need a "room where he can go to sleep and rest. While pet stores sell hamster "beds", you can just as easily – and less expensively – buy a small flowerpot or a small wooden box with an entrance hole for this purposes.

Indeed, you wouldn't feel at home if you didn't have some special items surrounding you. At the very least a few books, a television set, perhaps a few board of video games.

Well, your hamster needs some toys of his own. No, I don't think he'd be into video games – not his first few days at least. Your hamster's idea of games leans more towards exercise – no doubt about it.

First and foremost your new pet loves to run – he is in fact a serious runner. So the first item you'll want to put in the cage is a solid metal or a plastic exercise wheel.

But don't stop there. Place empty cardboard tubes from paper towels and toilet paper in the house as well. These make great tunnels for your friend to use. Climbing frames and seesaws can also keep your new friend occupied for a long time.

Hamsters are pretty cool creatures. Because they do insist on the creature comforts of life. Be sure to place small pieces of paper towels or napkins in the home as well. And don't be insulted if you discover that your new friend shreds these. That is exactly what you want him to do. He's making himself a nice, cozy nest to relax in after a strenuous workout in his wheel.

TAKING GOOD CARE OF YOUR HAMSTER

Welcome to the hospitality industry. With the adoption of your new pet and your purchase of his home, you've now become a hamster housekeeper of sorts. You must remember to remove his soiled bedding, droppings and uneaten food everyday.

You'll want to remove all the bedding and give the bottom of the cage a good washing. Rinse all the soapy residue off the cage. Then make sure – before your hamster goes back into his home – that everything is nice and dry before you place any new bedding down.

HAMSTER HOUSEKEEPING

Now that you've got the cage and the accessories, you'll need to know how to keep your new little friend healthy, happy and clean. This means you'll need some semblance of a schedule for cleaning his home.

Don't worry. Look at this place. Even if you bought the biggest hamster penthouse you could find, it isn't difficult – or that time consuming – to clean.

You'll discover that your hamster is the happiest and most energetic if you clean his "litter" area every day. Even if he hasn't eaten all his food, throw the old food out daily and give him fresh. (Look, it isn't that wasteful. We're talking about an animal that's barely 4 inches long. It's not a lot of food. It's like we're dealing with a Great Dane here!)

But in addition to that, make it a habit to completely change his bedding once a week. Once you have the old bedding out – and before you place the new bedding – give the cage itself a good scrubbing.

Hot, soapy water works best for this chore. Just be sure the entire surface is dry before you start replacing his bedding. He'll certainly appreciate this. And you can be assured that he's staying healthy.

Henry! Henry! Are you feeling alright? You don't look quite right. You've always wanted to run on that wheel before. Here, wear this ice pack on your head. Keep this thermometer in your mouth. I'm calling the vet. We'll have you up and running in that wheel again, gnawing on that toilet paper roll in no time at all.

Hmm. Got a sick hamster on your hands? We all feel a little under the weather now and then. Hamsters are certainly no exception to the rule. In fact, most hamsters display an illness with similar symptoms.

First, they'll just look different. They won't have the energy that they usually exhibit, they eyes won't have that shine. Not only that but if your hamster displays symptoms like shaking or looking weak, then it's a good bet he's not feeling well.

Other symptoms could include coughing an unusual gait and a stubborn cough as well.

Additionally, your hamster needs medical attention if his anus is smeared with droppings, noisy or heavy breathing, loose fur or patches of fur completely gone or sore spots on his body. Another symptom you want to look for in your hamster is dull-looking eyes.

If any of these characterize your ill hamster, then you need to call to make an appointment to see your veterinarian.

Even before you call your vet, though, you should take immediate steps to quarantine the individual hamster you suspect is ill. While his condition may not be contagious, if you keep him to himself immediately, then you won't need to worry about the others developing the same problem.

Along with this, give the cage a good cleaning. If it's at all possible sterilize all aspects of the cage. This could be as simple as placing these objects in water and boiling them for a minimum of 10 minutes. This should kill any germs.

Discard all bedding at this time and replace it with new. Don't forget the food. Throw all the uneaten food away. Replace it with fresh.

Wet Tail:
Even Without A Tail

While most of the time, a visit to the vet can clear up just about any health condition, there is one serious health problem you need to be vigilant about monitoring. The illness is simply called wet tail.

And yes, I know your hamster probably doesn't even have a tail. But his "rear end" will be wet. And you can certainly suspect that the bacteria called Lawsonia intracellularis is to blamed.

Technically, your vet calls it regional enteritis or proliferative ileitis. This illness is serious and it strikes mostly young hamsters of weaning age, between three and six weeks old.

Pay special attention to this possibility if you've adopted your hamster from a pet store. Those animals that are adopted here have just been weaned, so they're at the perfect age to develop it. But, hamsters of any age can contract this disease.

If your new hamster has wet tail, he'll appear lethargic – he'll be at a loss for energy – he won't want to eat and he'll stop grooming himself. Because of the severe case of diarrhea that accompanies this bacteria, his fur around the anus and tail will be matted, soiled and wet.

You can also tell by the look in the hamster's eyes that something is not well. The eyes will appear dull and sunken. The hamster affected with wet tail may sit "hunched up" (you'll know this as soon as you see this!) and he may be irritable. The irritability is quite understandable since he's in quite a bit of pain in this abdominal area.

If there's blood in your hamster's stool this could very well be an indication of this serious health condition.

Your hamster needs to see a veterinarian as soon as possible. She'll administer your little guy antibiotics to kill the bacteria. Additionally, she'll probably give him an intravenous dose of fluids as well as medicine to end the diarrhea.

Your little guy will also need to be kept warm and clean. The bad news is though that even with the best of treatment most hamsters die from this disease, most often as soon as 48 hours after they develop it.

Well, I'm sure you're asking now, what can I do to prevent this? Not much, unfortunately. You can't totally prevent wet tail, but you can decrease the risk of your hamster acquiring it.

Ensure that when you bring your new friend home his house is clean. Keep it as clean as possible. Wet tail occurs when the mother or other hamsters eat fecal-contaminate food or drink contaminated water.

Before you even adopt your hamster, ask your breeder if any of his relatives have ever had this disease. If you can, adopt your hamster from a lineage that has never been struck with this health condition.

Stress can also cause this condition. So to reduce your hamster's chances of developing wet tail, try to keep him as stress free as possible. This includes limiting the amount of time you handle them the first week they're in their new homes. You can also reduce your hamster's stress by keeping him on the same food that he had been eating. (If you do choose to change his diet, we've got tips for this in another chapter. There's a way to do that he won't even realize it's being done.)

Other common illnesses your hamster is susceptible to includes the common cold. It's a fact of life. You get them occasionally too. In fact, more than likely when your hamster does catch a cold, he'll get it from you.   Be sure to wash your hands before you handle your hamster or his food.

Symptoms of a cold in a hamster include a runny nose, sniffles, and general irritability. If you notice any of these signs, keep his home draft free. You also need to get him to a vet immediately.

Hamsters are also vulnerable to diabetes. If you think your hamster is urinating too much and drinking too much water, he may have diabetes. Other symptoms include lack of energy as well as weight loss. Additionally, his urine may attract ants.

If you suspect your hamster may be diabetic your vet can perform certain tests to confirm this.

THE COMMON COLD

It's an inevitable fact: Every living thing

gets the common cold at one time or another. And your hamster is no exception.

In fact, hamsters are quite susceptible to the common colds. You can help reduce the amount of cold by always washing your hands prior to holding your hamster. Most hamsters acquire their colds from people.

You can recognize when your hamster has a cold by the very symptoms of a runny nose, sniffles, and a general irritability (oh, yes, you'll be able to tell this last one!)

You need to two things immediately should your friend get a cold. First, you make sure he isn't exposed to any drafts and ensure that his cage is in a warm area of the home.

Second, call your veterinarian immediately to get him checked out.

Cuts and other wounds

Sometimes your hamster gets scratched – he may even end up with a bite or two. If this happens, you need place some antibiotic ointment on the wound. You'll want to hold your pet for about 10 minutes while the ointment sets in.

Perform this ritual daily for the wound until

it heals completely. If the wound is serious or gets infected, then you need to have a veterinarian examine it to see if it needs additional attention.

Ticks, bugs and other problems.

For the most part, you'll find that your hamster has very few skin problems. His fastidious habit of cleaning himself keeps his skin healthy. But you may discover that he occasionally has problems. It's possible that the cage may get some ticks or mites in it.

Usually, simply increasing your housekeeping efforts of his hamster condo can cure this problem rather quickly. If you discover that your hamster himself has mites on him, take him to see his veterinarian immediately.

Diabetes

Yes, we humans aren't the only creatures who are susceptible to diabetes. Your hamster may experience this disease as well. Some of the more common symptoms of diabetes in hamsters include a general lethargy, excessive drinking of water and associated urination. In addition, you may notice that his urine attracts ants.

As the disease progresses, you may even notice that your hamster is losing weight for apparently no reason. Just like if you suspected you had diabetes, you need to seek medical attention for your pet.

If you're curious, however, you can use strips that test for the presence of diabetes. These strips measure the glucose level in the urine. A high level of this sugar indicates that diabetes is probable. In turn that would definitely warrant a visit to the vet to for further tests to confirm these findings.

If the test is indeed positive then that would absolutely warrant a change in diet. You should feed your hamster a diet that emphasizes more complex carbohydrates, like broccoli as well as more protein, like millet, scrambled eggs and tofu.

Your veterinarian may also prescribe the drug Glipizide. This is an oral medication used to treat type 2 diabetes.

If the tests for diabetes come back negative, but your hamster is still urinating frequently and drinking water in seeming excess, consider the possibility he has a urinary tract infection.

If this is the case your veterinarian may prescribe an antibiotic. These may be either Baytril or Albon.

Many a hamster has been troubled by a puffy cheek pouch, caused by some material – either food or nesting material – impacted in this convenient natural carrying case.

If you don't get this treated, it could lead to an abscess. If you notice it early enough, you can try treating it yourself. Simply clean the cheek pouch with warm water. No, don't hold the poor guy under the faucet in your bathroom. Use an eyedropper to place the warm water on the sides of his mouth.

If you don't feel comfortable doing this, or you've tried this with no success, then make an appointment with your veterinarian. He'll be able to clean it in such a way as to not cause your hamster undue stress.

Yes, the teeth that never stop growing. You can help Henry Hamster keep his teeth healthy and well worn by ensure that a piece of hard wood is always within his reach. He'll take care of the rest.

For the most part, few problems occur with the teeth, but you may find an occasion or two to consult a vet. If a tooth has broken off, for instance, you should seek medical attention for him. Similarly, if his teeth are overgrown, take him to the vet.

CHAPTER EIGHT
TRUE HAMSTER LOVE . . .
And Beyond

It's time, so you think that Henry Hamster meets a Henrietta Hamster and have happy, little hamsters? Ah, before you decide with such certitude that you would like to breed these adorable creatures, you need to really think through the entire process in your mind. And perhaps even commit a game plan to paper.

Once your baby hamsters are born, for example, and weaned, just what are you going to do with them? If you're thinking that you're going to turn a quick profit selling them to your local pet store, think again. Many pet stores refuse to accept baby hamsters from the general public.

How many babies could possibly be in a litter of dwarf hamsters, you ask? After all the mom is so small herself. Well, the average size of a litter of pups ranges anywhere from four to six. But the Dwarf Campbell Russian Hamsters can have as many as 14 pups in a litter.

PLAN B?

Are you hoping to keep the babies – which by the way are called pups – for yourself? And if you are, do you have enough room for them? While they're a litter it's not too bad, but when they grow older they'll undoubtedly need to be separated to alleviate overcrowding in their home.

What if the hamsters become ill? Do you have the financial resources to provide them with the professional medical care they need?

Another possibility is that the mother may die following birth. This means that you're left holding the hamster baby bottle so to speak. Can you handle this responsibility – not only in the realm of knowing what to do, but financially and in terms of the time factor?

If you're planning on breeding hamsters, then you need to dig into the history of the offspring-producing hamsters. No, this isn't an invasion of privacy, it's solid research.

When you perform this research, you're specifically examining their genetic history. You want to know if anywhere in their past, any of their "ancestors" are carrying any defects or life-threatening illnesses that may pop up.

If you have a male and female hamster from a pet store, you probably don't want to breed these two little creatures. You are just about certain **not** to know enough about their health history to breed them responsibly.

In fact, ideally you should know enough about the two little furry creatures to say hat they are a good enough match to produce healthy, good-natured babies.

One of the aspects that you should consider is the size of your hamsters. Also, take into account the health of each animal as well as the temperament of the pair.

If you're interested enough in dwarf hamsters to breed them, then you already realize that each animal has a distinctive personality of their own. When you're matching up the hamsters, take this into account as well.

Don't even put the hamsters together until you've really looked at all the qualities of the pair – the good and the bad. These qualities are going to passed on to their babies.

You also want to pay special attention to the colors of the hamsters you're breeding as well. This may sound strange, but because of the specific genetic makeup of some hamsters, hamsters of certain colors should not be mated with others. Believe it or not, birth defects may occur.

TRUE HAMSTER LOVE:
THE MATING SEASON

If you're bound and determined to become a breeder . . . if you have a plan as well as a backup plan . . . then more power to you. We'll clue you in on a few of the basic facts of mating, breeding and raising dwarf hamsters.

You probably recall that hamsters become sexually at an incredibly young age by our standards. In fact, Henrietta hamsters have been known to be sexually mature as young as at four or five weeks. So much for the puberty years – your dealing with the puberty hour!

As a responsible breeder, though, you really don't want your female hamster pregnant at this age. She is far too young. Her giving birth at this age can result in some serious complications.

The best age to breed a female is at about four months of age. Once the female reaches the age of four months, you can put them in the same cage. But be careful how you introduce the two. Hamsters, the darling little things they are, do have some territorial issues. And when you're breeding them, you're going to need to respect them (even if you don't understand them!)

You can take the female and place her in the male's cage. Or you can place the couple together on some neutral territory. But don't place the male in the female's cage.

And your couple will take it from there. They'll sniff each other. You'll notice (if you must watch!) the female freezes in a distinctive position with her tail in the air. If the male hamster hasn't mated before, he may get a little confused at this point.

They won't know exactly what side to approach their potential mate from. The male will figure it out, even if he several first attempts fail and frustrate the waiting female. Curiously, a "virgin" female is much less tolerant of a "virgin" male than a female who has mated prior to this.

If the female is not receptive, then one of the two hamsters should be removed from the cage. And you'll know if the female isn't receptive, because they'll probably end up in a serious scuffle.

In fact, some experienced hamster breeders advise you to place the potential parents in a box. And they also advise you to wear gloves. If the pair isn't receptive then you'll be pulling the two of them apart because they'll be fighting. And you'll need the gloves to protect you from the clawing and the biting that is bound to ensue!

The mating "dance" and introductory time lasts for at least 20 minutes. You can't hurry this time. And yes, it is normal. As long as their sniffing each other and not fighting, leave the two alone.

If after one of the hamsters loses interest before the 20 minute period ends, then you definitely should separate them. You can return them to their separate cages.

If the male mounts the female, you can

keep them in the same cage until the birth of their offspring. If they begin to fight prior to the birth, then you need to separate them. Chances are though that they'll be just fine.

Female hamsters, being the nocturnal creatures that they are, come into season in the evening. They can stay in season for anywhere between four and 24 hours. A female is fertile for only the first year to 14 months of your life. But, evicentially, nobody has bothered to tell her that. She continues to come into heat even after she attains this age.

Right before they come into season, you'll notice a strong, musky smell. This is more noticeable in the summer. The day following her being fertile, the female discharges a thick, white substance from her vagina. This discharge can sometimes cause her urine to appear cloudy.

If your female doesn't get pregnant on the first try, she may come into season three days later.

Don't be disturbed if your female isn't fertile during the winter months. This is normal. If you would like to help Mother Nature a bit, you can artificially expand your hamster's hours of daylight by keeping a light on her for 12 hours a day for several days in a row. In addition to this you'll also want to feed her plenty of vegetables.

THINK THAT YOUR FEMALE'S IN HEAT?

So you think your female is ready to mate, but you're just not sure. You can discover this by simply firmly stroking her back starting with her neck and continuing to her tail. If she's in heat, she'll "freeze" in that position we described before with her tail pointed upwards.

If this occurs then you can put her with a male.

Sixteen days. If you've ever given birth – or been the "expectant father" – then you know how excruciatingly long nine months could be when you're waiting for you child to round out your family.

A hamster needs only to wait 16 days. Two weeks and two days! Imagine that! Sixteen days. Have I sufficiently expressed by amazement at this extremely short gestation period, as this period is scientifically called.

Well, let's be fair to some of those female

hamsters out there. Some other them don't actually give birth until their 17th or even their 18th day from the time of conception.

You probably won't notice any physical changes in your female hamster till about the 10th day of her pregnancy. At that time she'll "start to show". The tiny little abdomen becomes swollen while the nipples become more prominent.

From the time of mating, you need to assume that she is, indeed, pregnant. During these little more than two weeks of pregnancy, you'll wan to feed her high-protein foods. She appreciate scrambled or boiled eggs, wheat germ as well as tofu. You can even feed her a little peanut butter.

Be careful, though. Remember the size of this creature. It's easy to overfeed a pregnant hamster. You definitely don't want to do this.

And just because she's pregnant doesn't mean you shouldn't handle her. Show the little mother-to-be all sorts of love. Once she is several days away from the big day, you'll want to leave her alone – she'll appreciate the time to prepare. She'll also appreciate her privacy while she's nursing as well. During these two periods, the less contact you have with her, the better.

In anticipation of the new arrivals, you should clean the cage about two days before the due date. Make sure that your Henrietta has plenty of clean, suitable bedding.

You can recognize the birthing process, even if you've never seen a female hamster actually give birth before (few of us have, as a matter of fact!) When mom hamster begins to deliver, she'll place herself in a "hunched over" position. While in this unusual pose, she'll also move around quite a bit.

If you're really quiet and look very closely you may even see one of these very tiny babies actually being born. They may emerge head first, or they may come out feet first. It makes little difference to the ultimate health of the baby. So, relax, if you see one is coming out feet first.

Normally, hamsters deliver all their babies in the nest itself. However, sometimes nature isn't quite that tidy. She might have them in different areas of the cage. Don't let this worry you however, if she has spread her newborn family around the cage, she'll return to them to bring them all together.

Whatever you do, you don't want to touch her babies. The best action you can take once you see the pregnancy occurring is to leave her alone and keep the cage in a quiet room. If she knew how to talk, you're birthing mom would thank you for this.

In fact, you shouldn't touch the babies themselves until they're at least two weeks old. If you do, she might eat them. Yes, I know this sounds a bit harsh, but it is, however, a fact of hamster life. But once you touch them, those babies have your scent on them.

There are several other reasons why a mom may eat her young.

- If she was stressed by loud noises or by the father.
- The babies were born with a defect or a genetic disorder.
- If mom was a first time mom and inexperienced.

If this should happen, you may shy away from breeding your hamsters again. And understandably so. But don't. Let mom try again. The second pregnancy goes much smoother.

Mom, after all, now knows what's happening to her. Imagine giving birth to a little of tiny creatures for the first time when nobody has warned you what's happening with your body.

Normally, the second pregnancy will be much healthier, more of the litter survives and everyone is much happier all around.

If after 18 days of pregnancy, Henrietta still hasn't given birth, you can just about safely assume that she had a phantom pregnancy, or that there were problems with either the labor or with the birthing process itself.

One of your options is to take the mom-to-be to the vet to induce labor. Doing this with a dwarf hamster is extremely difficult. Few vets are willing to do this.

You don't need to worry about the status of the unborn babies though. The fetuses are normally just re-absorbed into the mother's bloodstream. As strange as this may sound, it's really quite normal. And of most importance to you, it causes no health problems to the mom.

If, however, you can see that Henrietta is having visible problems giving birth, or if she's showing any physical indications that she's ill, then take her into the vet's to have him look at her.

Congratulations! You're about to be "grandhamster parents." Yes, this is a very touching moment in your life. What you may not realize it, your life is about to change. If you think having two dwarf hamsters is fun, wait till you start caring for an entire family.

A newborn hamster is very small, pink, hairless, deaf and blind. And small, did we say small? Like three grams weight-worth of small? Yes, he's small!

What's not to love about these tiny babies?

Their tiny little eyes can barely be seen under their skin (but don't worry, the eyes are definitely there as you'll see shortly).

And surprisingly, unlike human babies, these little ones are born with teeth. This allows them to suckle. And what a spectacular sight that can be for you. At birth, the skin of a baby hamster is actually

145

transparent. So if you can catch a glimpse of drinking milk from his mom, you actually can see the milk travel from his mouth to his stomach!

Despite the size, the looks and the apparent lack of senses on the part of the babies, Henrietta Hamster loves her new little ones fiercely. She'll take good care of them. If your hamster is of the Campbell species, you can expect to have about six new little hamsters.

If your hamsters are of the other species you can expect to see anywhere from one hamster to up to 14.

CARING FOR THE BOUNCING BABY HAMSTERS

Mom is busy nursing. Look how proud she looks. Oh, no! A mom hamster should never be disturbed while she's nursing. You can't even go in there to clean the cage at this point. (But don't worry, as you'll recall, these little guys mature super fast!).

You may be tempted to help "re-arrange" the pups for her. In order to feed them properly, she'll no doubt end up laying on her babies. This will not harm them. In fact, it helps them to stay warm.

When Mom does leave to eat or perform those other necessities in life, she'll cover them with bedding or shavings. If she does this, you may not be able to see them at all (she is a private hamster, now isn't she?). But don't worry, you'll definitely hear them squeaking for her return.

MOM'S HAMSTER HABITS

If your hamster has given birth before she reached the age of four months, she may be more prone than an older hamster to actually neglect her children. In some instances, very young mothers also reject or even eat they young.

These young moms are confused – both physically and mentally – by the entire birthing process (aren't we all?). If your particularly hamster is very young when she gives birth, then you want to make sure that you do your level best not to disturb her at all. You want to provide her with every chance of taking care of them.

But even older hamsters sometimes "cull the litter." A mom may reduce the number of pups in her litter to more manageable levels for her. Studies have actually been done on this phenomenon. It shows that a mom will reduce the size of the litter in a smaller group to insure that proportionally more males are there. If the litter is larger, than mom makes sure that more females remain in the family.

As your mom hamster continues to feed her young, you'll want to make sure that you continue to feed her those high protein foods which are so necessary in helping her provide her babies with nutrition.

The skin of the babies become either dark or flesh colored between four to six days after birth. Around the fifth day after birth and continuing on to the seventh, you'll notice that the hair of these new arrivals begins to emerge. Also during this time period, the ear open.

By nine to 10 days of age, the babies are covered in short fur. Their eyeballs are developing as well. You'll also notice that the eyelids are beginning to develop.

Even though the babies are still blind, they may during this time, start roaming about the cage. It's a sight to see, because the mom picks them up and returns them to the nest! It's a cute game of "But, Mommy, I want to see the world!"

At two weeks to 16 days, the eyes of the newborns are now open. The babies are also completely covered in fur. And now, finally, when all this occurs, you can safely start handling them. But only for short periods. And really only to clean the nest

These youngsters are also ready to eat "solid" food. You can feed them some grated carrots, wheat germ and perhaps a scrambled or boiled egg.

As they grow, you'll also feed them the commercially produced food, especially those that are rich in protein.

THREE WEEKS OLD

Finally, your young brood is three weeks old. They're fully weaned. And that's a good thing. They are no longer in need of Mom's milk. But no one has actually informed the little guys of that. If Mom still has milk left, then they'll still suckle on her.

Now is the perfect time to separate the babies from Mom. And for that matter the baby boys from the baby girls. That's right! You'll need two more cages (one for the girls and one for the boys).

Moving the babies from their mom no doubt is stressful for the little guys. But don't discount the fact that this initial separation can be just as stressful for Mom as well. She'll need several days to adjust to her empty nest.

NOW WHAT TO DO WITH THE BABIES?

You'll want to keep the babies with their siblings for another two to three weeks before you place them in their individual living quarters. And you'll still want to feed these maturing young pups high-protein foods. After all they are still growing.

While they're separated from Mom, don't hesitate to handle them. This makes the adjustment period in their new homes just a little bit easier.

Once they hit five weeks of age, you can confidently adopt these guys out to good loving homes.

You've done a good job of raising your hamsters! Ready to try it all over again?

152

Conclusion

The dwarf hamster is a unique animal. It makes little difference whether you discover the feral type in his natural habitat or you encounter the domesticated version.

You can't argue with the fact that he's a cute, furry creature who is sure to bring a smile to your face.

But the questions remains: Is he the right pet for your family?

Only you can answer this question. His tiny size make him an ideal addition to a family who lives in an apartment. But don't allow his small stature lull you into believing that he doesn't need the love and attention that you would give any other pet – like the family dog or cat!

Because he does! He would like nothing better to get to know you – on his terms though. Befriending the dwarf hamster is not an achievement that you'll accomplish in a day. You've probably already discovered this from some aspects of this book.

But when you do gain his trust and affection, you'll learn that a whole new world has opened up – not only to you, but also to your little friend!

If you do decide to adopt your very own dwarf hamster, keep that "love" aspect in mind. But also remember that he needs the medical attention of a professional veterinarian. A recent survey showed that only a mere five percent of dwarf hamster owners actually take their pets to a vet. This is a must if you want him to live the two and half or three years of his life healthy and happy.

The advantages of loving a dwarf hamster is that the necessary accessories that accompany his place in your heart and home are relatively inexpensive. You'd be amazed at how affordable a great condo is for him as well as the cost of the various toys that he'll need to keep him busy.

Yes, owning a dwarf hamster could be a

very good thing indeed.

So, when is Henry coming home with you?

19179327R00083

Made in the USA
Lexington, KY
10 December 2012